I0149983

Carolyn Steinhoff's poems have appeared in *Book of Matches, Global Poemic, The Indypendent, Cape Rock, And Then, House Organ, Emerge Literary Journal, The Hat, Conjunctions* and many other journals and publications. Her chapbook, *Plain English*, and her play, *The Setting Face to Face with the Clear Light*, were published by Texture Press. She has had nonfiction articles in numerous magazines including *Multicultural Review, Ae3U: America's AIDS Magazine*, and *Today's Latino Magazine*, for which she was a staff writer. She published the paper magazine of art and writing, *From Here: Sex, Politics and Power*, was a recipient of the Jingle Feldman Award for Performance from the Tulsa Arts and Humanities Council, and has received grants from the Oklahoma Arts Council, the MidAmerica Arts Alliance and the Puffin Foundation.

History of the Future

Carolyn Steinhoff

Published by Nauset Press

nausetpress.com

Wareham, MA

Cover and Book Design: Nauset Press
Cover Illustration: Copyright © Kaori Serakaki, Artist, Okinawa Institute of Science and Technology Graduate University
https://www.oist.jp/ja

ISBN: 979-8-9859692-6-9
Library of Congress Control Number: 2022949874

Grateful acknowledgement is made to the publications in which some of these poems first appeared:
A Dead Country in Your Head, *The Indypendent*
Love Bubbles, *Global Poemic*
Cosmic Dentistry, *Book of Matches*

for Benny and Enzo

Contents

So Little

. . . the Milky Way and ever larger stars and suns
make what we are seem so little.

–Ingeborg Bachmann

Every night, their light white-cold in the summer heat,

the streetlights shine on ones fleeting and breakable

as the streets under our feet, and on the leaves

layering their shadows on shadows over the sidewalks,

flat and alive, transparent, made to restlessly

dart and dodge over and under each other like a pack of thieves

by the summer wind. To shimmy over my skin

as if they wanted to get under it, as if they were the shadows of age

or illness instead of the shadows of leaves, and the lines they made

      across my face

were words in a book a white-haired old man was holding,

a god we had invented to worship,

who held our lives open in his hands

and was underlining every line on every page

and writing big asterisks next to each paragraph

and writing our fates down in the blank spaces

at the end of every chapter in an illegible scrawl,

like the handwriting of an old doctor. As I walk under the sky,

under the lights, and the leaves write their shadows on my clothes,

and somewhere the innocent sleep, and birds close their vaulted wings,

and each step of mine presses the earth hard,

my movement is toward my own place,

toward being a filament, status-less,

because we've mistakenly seen ourselves as so little.

Silences I Remember

I worked on my speech for years,
the one where I explain
the death I want to have, and the day came
for me to deliver it.
The lights went down on the audience,
up on me. I could see nothing
but bright light. I cleared my throat
and presented it without notes.
"I've thought for a long time
that I don't want to be a burden on you.
'As soon as I don't recognize you,' I've said,
'let me stop eating and drinking.' But then,"
I explained, "I learned about how people
can enter the world of the lost. The lost love it.
So I ask you if you would enter my world
when I become lost." There was silence
in the hall. The lights came up. Somehow
the audience had quietly departed.
That's what I
most remember, that I was
again the poem drinking from itself.

Same Old New Types of Silence

I will the mother they want to take over my body.
I want the way it was for white people to keep being the way it is
but now there are as many ways it is
as there are splinters in the plywood floor. There are now
       splinter groups.
Groups that are no joke, if one gets under your skin.
It's not funny when hungers get under your skin.
They can't be expected to walk naked along the cobblestones
or drive on the highway exposed. They have to clothe themselves
so why not in a body? In this same old new world a body easily
becomes a despised thing. What is it for hungers to inhabit
white people while facts loll around on the sidelines like cartoons?
Imaginary conversations proliferate now, as real ones
become dangerous. What is a country anymore even?
Talk about it to your imaginary boyfriend.
What is a president? A language even anymore? Well,
      you can say to him,
language sits up there like a moon.
You can say a country is a large pinkish dish in the night in which
we can watch our Selves being forged before and above our eyes,
from which bodies are then proffered in the pink bowl
of the country for us to put on. Thanks. Now I lug around
this fatter, this heavier thing, this thing so old and sickened
I don't recognize it. This language that's so thickened
that even calling a day beautiful can make us cry now. Because this
kind of beauty in this month should not be. Feeling the exhausted,
alien body taking the lightning again in this particular month
can make people so exhausted it should not be. While at home

the silence that should be carved out of the noise

of a family is keen and deep,

because there is no hubbub waiting behind it to resume.

Because silence as the baseline you stop staving off

and completely give in to is not what you want.

You want a life so noisy that silence is a relief

not a life so silent that hearing voices is a relief. Hearing them

     talk to you

as if you're the mother they want is a relief.

Vanishing Point

Each new silence
—call not returned, fact left out—
might take me a step deeper
into the scary forest of the fairy tales,
dark, soughing, with its hummocks
of monumental trunks fallen, returning to the mother,
leaving pits where creaking root worlds were buried
until they thrust themselves up to the air.
Each silence rooted out could be a bite,
by the wolf of existence at my heels,
a bite of emptiness I'm swallowing,
that's lifting me like a balloon let go of
into the sky of my dear old self pressing me on all sides
to hold the molecules of my name inside.
Or maybe each new silence shoots me, like a car,
closer to the point
the lit, building-lined avenues vanish into.
Somewhere past my quiet, prettified body
going about its duties, the self trying to conform
is naked. In some deep sky
the silences should start to disappear.

What *To Be* Means

To be means *to exist.*
So in 2021 stay at least as alive
as you already are.
Keep up the ins and outs
of breathing. *To exist* means
to not let one's breath be taken.
Yes, the lungs seize with each dunking
in each moment that hits the body like ice water,
it's true. When, among all one's acquaintances,
one's ears are the only ones uncovered,
the ones hearing the people,
muffled as their cries are
by their cocoons of darkness,
then *to be* means that to keep up
the shaking of the numbed by the lapels
is exhausting. When a book
loved since childhood
is suddenly missing its pages,
then to sustain the body,
to organize records and string words like beads
—these acts become
the emptiness between covers
that replaces time.
That the books that surround are faded,
that the pages that remain are brittle,
means the words bided their time
like birds one kept tamed by one's will.
They have broken free.

To surrender means the moment

has no borders

so time races away.

History of the Future

. . . the only way of perpetuating a love that we do not want to abandon.

—Sigmund Freud

I want to think that, in my apartment,

with the colors, the layout, the furniture,

the plates and wine, I can box back grief.

But death snuggles against my sleeping form

to get warm

so when I wake to another day

yawning around me

like a shrunken stretched-out pocket

and I feel death there,

I have to lie so so still;

then death climbs

into my cells and prowls,

looking to take hold.

Just as branches struggling and pitching

are the way we know the wind is in trees,

when death blows through our species,

stories of bodies falling

somewhere out there

are all that reveal its passage.

I want to keep terror at the windows

but death lifts my roof like a lid

so I fly from my body—

look, that mask down there is my face—

I fly back, seek to occupy myself,

all I've learned about love that's left me,

a woman clutching a rag

that once was her favorite doll.

While way out on the Isle of the Abandoned,

white suited figures carve trenches,

stack hundreds of thousands of longish white boxes in them,

throw on shovelful after shovelful of dirt.

American

It's only when you're on top of the world,

astride a country invincible as a raptor,

with a name bestowed on you—*American*—

without which you would ask in panic "Who am I?"

and you see your own future, if you don't hold on,

in those ragged, sick, starving ones

shuffling through snow on swollen feet;

when you watch beloved characters

in your stories from a dead century

impale themselves on the razor wire you're just noticing,

that winds around the periphery;

it's only then, when your country's suddenly slowed by a bullet

it scavenged from a dead disobedient

and resold at a markup,

it's then you understand

that the name's like a triangle tattooed on your arm

that you woke up with from a drugged sleep in a strange place;

that you're not on the country's back

but in its claws.

That your life is continuing—

like everyone's—

at a wounded predator's whim.

The Favorite

He maketh me to lie down . . .
—THE BIBLE, New Kings James version

"I am the favorite," the crowned man,
the uniformed man is always saying.
His power is that, to save their skins,
the shoeless act like his lies are true.
A word against him
sits trapped in their mouths;
when their mouths open
and the word does not fly out
then its weight on their tongue
makes staying awake suddenly
seem impossible to them;
then sleep is a memory from childhood.

When a mother loves a child so much
she carries her over mountains
and deserts barefoot
to deliver her from evil
the one in the crown, in the badge so envies them
that he shakes the earth in slow motion.
When he orders the bonds
microscopically examined
and sees how they are unconditional,
how they are constant,
how he is not her favorite,
then as gradually as the flower
folds back its petals,

shows its black center,

as gradually as that he has to break the planet.

As slowly as the mother

who can only notice the fire

by turning away from the house

turns back later and sees ruins,

that slowly, he wakens the birds

asleep in flight

so they fall from the sky,

the dolphins swimming in their sleep

so they drown. When the mother holds her dear life

to the sun like seeds

he has them scattered on stones.

Has her children to lie down

chained, in the bowels of her memory,

counting each child he uses to destroy her

with a tally mark in his Victory column.

First she stands in the black carbon rain,

her face to the sky,

her arms stretched up,

her word shooting from her mouth to space.

Next she gathers the black drops

and the primal non-sound into a dot

and swallows it.

Next she makes her way to a desk

and allows the infinitely tiny

infinitely dense mass to roll out.

A Dead Country in Your Head

In a country where they're trained to shed
old women like out-of-fashion coats
a Self has to be a container for everybody's No,
the sole repository of knowledge
about where you come from and where you go,
a holder of a dream, where you belonged
with some people, that you can be trying to remember;
trying to remember it makes you forget it
so you stop trying and that makes you forget the dream.
In the same way, for years you can be resuscitating
a dead person or country in your head and not know it
or you can feel the life you're living
is a false life without realizing it.
The past can come to seem
as if it's sending you some natural light,
into the dark dead air
of your big-city apartment. Some laughing
and hugging can exist in your memory,
which is the limbic system of your brain,
as closed as a defunded library
full of books sitting there aging, like grief
sitting there nice and neat on the shelves of the Self.
In the same way the huge No that's said and unsaid,
that lives in us, can sound louder to us than the clatter of glass
and plastic recycling the superintendent is handling
in the no-space between the buildings,
louder than a drill groaning like a beast,
that some people are using to renovate

an emptied apartment next to you to rent at a profit.

In a country like that

words of love coming to you out of the ether seem like angels.

Feed Love

To those saying *I love you* to you,
feed love, like water into leaves;
give them a threshold you can carry them over
into feeling. Together you might form
an undulating being there,
which holds itself to the sun,
feels the moon unknowable as bones
pulling on it, casts shadows to wriggle
ungraspable as thoughts over the lawn,
slipshod upending things, thoughts.
What do they do to you with their language?
Words tiny as grains
embed in the soul's lining like a thousand eyes,
able to see in the wrinkled petals of old roses
the folding up of the seas,
able on waking to silence to see darkness
that never ends. Soul sessile as grass,
confer upon yourself a quiet.
Read my mind aloud to yourself
in your rooms. While I try to keep my limbs out
of the grinder of the generations,
my face out of the wind
stirring the masses like a fever
to cheering and chanting in the stands.

Words R Us/Bodies R Us

Her stunt double doesn't care
about syntax, propriety or marketability,
only about letting what tears in her find its way
out and find a home. Only about the answer
to her question: Am I a box,
taped up and thrown next to a highway
in rural Oklahoma, or am I the words
clawing and whining like puppies inside?
Her stunted double takes her place
in that future where her mind would go
if it refused to stay there in the box.
She waits for the answer until hair grows
from her old chin like cornsilk,
one to a kernel. Like the spindly young trees
in the endless forest that shall cover the new earth
after the salted ocean of words
that is drowning our cities
rises over them from inside of them.

Love Pulls Itself Apart

There is thunder in the heaven
under our feet. Doors to the trains there part;
people run out, like salt. If people come in,
the doors close. If no one comes in,
the doors close. Over our heads
a small transparent cloud pulls itself apart,
the way love does. Now it is February.

Yet the sun pummels the plants and planets,
the cement and hats, the keepers of speech
who speak to the parts of us that want our speech kept.
If I cannot keep the world,
then I want the world to keep me.
I want the parts of me
left out in the sun
to be kept. I want the melted, soured parts of me left out
of the refrigerator to be kept—
I think everything about me
should be valuable. I crave the world on a string.
Or if I cannot have it
then I want to be the string.
Then I want the world to have me.
I long to ride out with it
on the blizzard as on a bullet train,
to go where it takes me,
round bends, up and up and then
down
like lightning

into the valley,

Whee!

To be set down finally

into the apartment I live in where,

behind me, furniture romps in silent glee,

holds momentous summits

at which the fate of the world is decided,

then rushes back into place

when I turn around. All I see is a glow.

The speech keepers

who've burrowed into my soul

cannot control what happens to them there.

While they scritch-scratch away in the depths,

I caper to and fro, hither and yon

over the crust of beautiful stories

that lies over the top of the whiteout.

Between the baby cedars

that hunch round-shouldered in the front yard

wearing their caps of snow.

Cosmic Dentistry

"I feel my dreams dragging me into them
even as I brush my teeth," he said.
Knowing he will dream that the woman he loves
is a wolverine makes him not want to go to sleep.
And knowing that when he wakes up without her
he'll look ugly and tired instead of rested and handsome
makes him not want to wake up.
His life, in a bowtie and tux,
used to pull him along behind it.
He, in his red velvet bellbottoms,
could barely keep hold of its coattails.
Now that he and his life walk side by side,
both in t-shirts and jeans, holding hands,
he feels he should be able to dream of perfect teeth.
It seems to him the city of his dreams
should halt its hollowing out.
More and more cocoons for the rich spring up,
to release the owners of the streets
onto the streets he walks. When the world becomes
this sort of bubble, people sharp as himself
become the enemy. "May your kiss
always be just a kiss,"
he prays to the savior of his dreams,
"not a mark pointing me out to the squads. If your magic words
are knit of wool, then pull them over a monster's eyes."
He envisions his unprotected love speech
bursting from his mouth,
inseminating the community with his ideas and desires.

He vows his thoughts will never languish

in a brain dead as stone teeth in heaven's mouth.

"Let me not be a smear of dust on the fingers

of a conveniently invisible god."

In Front of You

Wavelengths fill the world but lie outside our senses . . .
—Carl Safina

Sound waves slinky waves transverse waves light waves jump rope

waves mechanical waves seismic waves water waves pressure waves

gamma rays x rays alpha waves neutron waves beta waves infrared

radio microwaves visible waves. What is in front of you

is a catalogue made of light waves,

of tiny pictures of food and dresses that are for sale,

that takes all the neuronal waves you can muster

to make sense of.

Teachers are in front of you like slinky waves

following the status quo around,

like the domesticated animals they are.

Their voices have escaped as sound waves,

unnoticed, into the river, rendering them mute,

like guest workers interchangeable as pronouns,

so now they open their wallets to just about anyone,

bent as they are on winning hearts and minds and the lottery.

O Reader, keeper of the Visa and the Amex cards,

predictor of foreseeable futures,

teach yourself to feel the jump rope

waves in front of you we pray, the bulletin board,

the battered, cumbersome dictionaries.

To register the words

loping by in asymmetrical lines of pressure waves,

peeking out like Easter eggs from under a pile of notes

passed in class, heaped by the door. The moment expands

in neutron waves around Kings County like Spanx

and holds it tight and secure. Inside it seismic wavelengths
thrill through me, make my skeleton hum, like the sonar
of highly advanced animals. They torture and kill people,
you know, for harboring this sort of communication
in the dusty attics of their souls. They laud people
running for office for killing this kind of boundlessness
before it can throw the very planets off their orbits,
blowing out volcanoes like birthday candles so our wish
not to be immortalized in lava like the Pompeiians
can come true. O outlandish spectacle of mechanical waves
washing through every body, making pictures in the brain,
restore me to the moment vast and corrupted as the seas,
O crowds of wavelengths galloping wholesale through the world.

Superstition

Some say it has always been there on the far side
of the Sea of Existence I've been riding around on
in my body, full of deserving, like one of these ubiquitous
container ships out for a spree, zigzagging off their courses,
carrying cargos in and out of the days, nights full of losses and secrets,
valuable explosive lies in the hold, crated in sawdust so they won't break
open anyone's world. The plays are already underway on the decks,
though the pretend selves are still putting on their costumes
down below. I am distracted from them by the storms,
by excitements jumping around me like flying fish eyeing me,
silver, mercurial as a happy conversation.
No father or agèd friend says any shore has been sighted.
Are they keeping it to themselves?
Is it impossible to describe? Is seeing it like a religious experience?
Maybe they're too busy navigating shoals and reefs, like everyone,
to see it appearing as if out of nowhere on their horizon.
Who among us can believe they have been going toward it
without knowing it, without wanting to know it,
since they coalesced out of the ether as a person with
        their own personality?
I can imagine dead friends and relatives beckoning
        to me from somewhere
but nonexistence is a netherworld Shangri La we all talk about
but have never had an eyewitness report of.
A future without me in it. We all know that's impossible to believe.

Clouds of the Near Future

I know the clouds over New York will look funny tomorrow
because I read it in a terrestrial almanac I came across
by accident, that someone had left in a surrey I passed
as I was listening to the city creaking around me
like icebergs breaking up, in one of my waking dreams.
I know these clouds will be like nothing anyone has seen.
They will be discrete, steel-blue, wavy-edged ovals.
Each will be outlined in gray, some of the smaller ones
so thickly they will be almost all gray,
with only a thin line of blue in the middle.
Like a member of some disappearing species,
like a banded bird or something
trying to leave a trace of itself,
in the wee hours of the day the climate will pin
each of these fake-looking cutouts carefully,
covertly against a dirty background
which will finish above the towers as messy white piles
mushrooming into classic azure. Yes, there will be blue sky,
but it will have nothing to do with the silly
flattened circles down below. When I told
the dreadlocked top-hatted minstrel who
from time to time accompanies me
on my commutes with his guitar
and his rhymes about Al Qaeda how it is
that I am privy to this information,
he didn't believe me.

Hand in Glove

At first I wanted to be the hand
and I wanted you to be the glove.
I wanted to be the room,
whose walls you, the one bird sound,
would penetrate.
I wanted to be the wind
and you to be the cloud
I moved and reshaped and dispersed.
You to be the planet
always turning your good side
to me, your ball of fire,
me your blinding white tunnel waiting for you
to step into. Then it was revealed
that you were the wind and also the cloud
and the hand and also the glove
and the fire and the planet and the sound and the
charming but silent and windowless room
and so was I.

The Boy Is Getting Up

Wedded to his life,
taken out of a drawer of sleep
by this day as old as the earth,
the boy is the same boy but unfolded,
atoms of his grandparents
stirring in his skin
in a way never before seen,
layering a pink color on him
over the dull old sadness.
"Nice to see you again, Day,"
he is sighing. "We are altered, you and I,
I from the sleeping, the dreams,
you from the turning,
the affair between our earth and sun."
She is his Day; he is her boy,
he and the grass and squirrels
and the other people,
and the deaths on this spot of earth
never before seen, last breaths
of the new dead, added to her.
In the midst of their season
each leaf and blade whispers to her,
"You are all I ever wanted, you
and your breezes.
Thank you for coming back,
you and your other side, Night."
This morning the smell of rain,
of decay that is making its way

through the bricks and glass
into the cages, the rooms,
tells him it is his Day
that is mother to him now,
father to those lifting their limbs.
"Why do you sigh
and cry for us?" the dry leaves,
the cold loves are asking. "Changes
are in your blankets and drawers,
in your cups and tears."
The world is alive
in front of and around him
and knows how to hide
it from him. He is rubbing
his eyes, shaking out
his foolish costumes
to see what grains,
what grains of what
might be hiding in their folds.

What Was

What was leaves its mark

What can the body want for,

with all that lives in its folds?

As the point

into which all the world's histories vanish,

what can the body not know?

Passed through by every wave,

even the hiss eons have smoothed

the Big Bang into,

what does the body not hear?

Electrified as it is with the same currents,

pulled on by the same moon

that impelled that first fish

to shuffle out of the sea,

the body driven by the question,

Who can I be?

lurches like a hunted unbeliever

taking refuge in a professing church on Sunday,

like little Darwin stumbling

onto "powerful young men about six feet high." [1]

The question carries the body along,

the lightest animal riding a breeze;

the message, like a new way to breathe,

that people are not rooms

but wildernesses, carries the body along.

"I cannot be a place with walls

that you can set up residence in

and decorate." The body is stopped

by patterns—beliefs, ways to hate—
as unalterable-seeming as seasons,
patterns that are stricken, that are fallen
and are in shambles,
that are lying like monstrous trees
fallen across its path.

[1]   THE VOYAGE OF THE BEAGLE —Charles Darwin

Now That

Being remembered is very often confused with being loved.
—Apoorvanand

Now that the face is nothing to anyone but a video,
its atoms rearrange themselves from the inside,
according to the owner's thoughts,
now that they're not pressed anymore
by the other's gaze.
Now that the body always lies alone,
its longing rises to meet it,
hard and consuming as the floor it lies on.
Feet pressed the earth last year,
mine among them,
intent to be met not swallowed
but one by one some were taken,
one by one then by the thousands,
by the hundreds of thousands and now
we open Earth's mouth
and force our dead down her throat.
Did we want the face to be all ours,
the floor, the earth to concede?
"Our Earth," the rats say,
become bold as they eat their young.
"Ours," say the last rhododendron buds
dark as viscera, sharp as flames
on the clusters of opened flowers,
the last on earth still closed to the sky
that sags over them like a blanket about to tear
with the weight of all the dead.

In this lunging of the state toward us subjects

where does the tiny old stripped-down woman,

steeped in want, lodge,

who thought she was running to nowhere but then—

nowhere has run to her?

Heaven's angels are cutouts in this place,

decoys she followed into the chamber

whose doors the tyrant closed behind her

and locked from the outside.

Here I am the single sparrow

who was invisible until the wind

roused a small red tree from its stillness

and it shook me out.

What Absence Was

Her head was a mountain;
absence was like water
dripping onto it,
making caverns so deep inside
their only visitors were the
blind things who lived there.
Absence was a red letter
embroidered across her face
in invisible thread. Absence
was the end of a tale so long
no one could finish telling it.
Absence was a secret
she would take to the grave.
The god of her people did not forbid it;
too busy trolling for souls—to save!!
Absence was like gravity,
holding her down, not expected
to wear off. It was quotidian,
as innocent as breath.

A Life of Peace

In the body of air and water she's been assigned
she wanders the city clothed in nothing
but the lies her mother told her about herself,
the lies the bosses tell about the poor.
They are fitted over her bones
like a skin suit.
The devil has her by its sleeve.
He makes her walk with him
over the sidewalks:
"Smile to my admirers," he hisses.
"Tell them I am your friend."
Her life is a ladder
leaning on mist.
There is no shortcut
to the place called stillness.
There is no long way round.
Her eye is on that beach up there
where the reading of poems
is all that shatters the day.
She carries that future in her skull
since no words invented can talk her into
a life of peace. No one's invited her
to be alive in the body she's given.
So she's the devil's plus one
at the world's costume party.
She goes as King of the Invisibles.
All the guests there feel her emotions

about the end of truth

stinging them.

Not Discovered

I am the last lake not discovered.
Its surface sparkles there between the mountains
while some conclusion is reached
with no one to see, deep in my body, love I feel
sitting at the bottom breathing
like the giant squid in Lake Baikal,
five thousand feet down.

The Time of the Mountain

'I'm all of them, I'm Romi and Juli, I'm a mebfil, *I'm a gathering. Of everything and nothing. Is there anyone else you'd like to invite? Everyone's invited.'*

—THE MINISTRY OF UTMOST HAPPINESS, Arundhati Roy

What do you become,

when the dreamed-of, longed-for,

lived-for imaginary remembered love chatter

is more real to you than the silence you live?

You become nothing. You become everything.

You become each moment

and the stone that moment turns into.

When the no longer existing next moment

hovers motionless as a curtain of gauze,

thin as old skin, what do you say?

You say nothing. You say

everything; you say

I am this. Of the book AFTER DARK,

last opened on a day receding farther and farther

from the day of this writing which is itself now past,

and the book LIVE OR DIE, dusty and askew among a thousand

dusty books; of the painting, whose freight of memories

can't be unloaded, a self-portrait of a girl in blue, reading,

—your daughter the painter

  with you on your Italy trip—

of the invisible memory train running

from the clay vases on your shelves

that she and her sister made

in their childhoods, of all this you say

I am this to no one. *This peony*

a stranger gave me on Mother's Day, you say,

the white ball of it shy as I was with my first boy;

this bud I thrust into the tap water it's taking into its stem,

that powers the folding back of its petals;

the petals unwrapping in slow motion

like arms from around a body,

baring the red at their base;

the mute face of it lifting itself to me,

the yellow stamens wormy inside;

the ragged inmost petals, the inebriating scent—of this you say

I am this to the silence. You say,

This is not the time of the mother but the time of the flower.

Not the time of a body but the time of the soul.

This is not the time of human beings

but the time of the mountain.

You can watch a bud all night,

clenched and alive and not alive,

to see it open itself by morning.

Or you can you distract yourself with cooking

or war in the streets while the flower changes.

Changes such as this, such healing and dying,

you cannot see,

except by looking away. *This change,*

you say to everyone, *of this dead flower: I am this. I am*

not this.

Love Bubbles

Evil is possessed, unlike mere misery,
of a dark glamour nobody pities.
—Franz Wright

Discover where the Lost Men,
JA, James B, Muddy, the others,
got their freedom and courage:
this is the assignment given
to certain members of the populace
chosen for their formlessness.
Their mission: put together
a tutorial on how to distinguish
between pitiful unhappiness
and glamorous evil, unhappiness's
"most successful disguise."
But the invisible shepherd
has driven this domesticated segment
into a pen called Distraction,
where they can't work,
where the distinct ones,
who could once be stroked and punched,
who have never killed
their consciousness, their longing
for love that never comes,
have been rendered as 30-second
on-demand videos and shares
that no one shares or demands.
Words of love now leave their mouths
as bubbles the wind carries off and breaks.

When the words were sounds,

they acted like a hall of sound

down which the vague and precise alike

could stroll, between walls of sound

that neither reached to them

to entice them to stay forever,

nor spooked them into getting out

as fast as they could. Now, as bubbles

streaming forth and popping, their songs

create a festive atmosphere for the dying,

while the figures of the living

are being unraveled,

their ideas pulled from inside them

like a thread from a sweater.

The Lost peek out from behind a bush

in the wilderness. *Are we horrible or sad?*

the shaky white masses ask of them,

as they fill the once empty apartments

and pine for a cuddle. Here is how

you sort out the difference:

the Idea, justice for all, whose neck

is under the boot of the baby-man with the scepter,

wrests free and holds up a torch,

while the lowly shepherd cries

in a tearful tangle and we comfort them.

Forgetting the Words

When you read or sing
and the act pulls you
through a long narrowness
into the arms of emptiness,
can you really let words wing through
like birds across a sky?
Can you watch longing
glide like a far-off boat,
your being proving nothing?
When none of the flowers
surrounding me are alive—
some are silk; some are dried—
the sky is a shock; the light it sends
strikes my body.
Space stretches its jaws
over me, with everyone
having pulled their walls close
around them like a shawl,
a bullet-proof shawl,
as the constant effort of forgetting
subsumes them
in spite of themselves.
It's like when you're on a ledge
high over a city
or a valley
and a voice in you says, "Jump"
or you're on a highway
and feel you'll turn the wheel

and take an unfamiliar exit
that will get you lost forever.
You think, "What if I forget, too?
That I am equal?" Can you not find
that you've become a destroyer, too?

Inventory

What I have:

- The best apartment I can afford

- This family

- Today's categories to live in: Old. White. Woman. Old Woman

- The shallowness and the questing of this and of every time

- Perceptions stored up in clogs in the heads
  until people wake up with headaches

- These fantasies of freedom the brains make
  releasing like chemicals into the collective bloodstream

- The narrow path that is given

- This one dot of a body to remain poised in
  between here and there, ecstasy and sorrow,
  no personality to be inserted,
  beholden to its own blood

How to Hide in Our Bodies

It was a huge man
who lit me in my dream
when I was three;
I clutch the comfortable old fire
like a beloved doll
I secretly still sleep with.
When I was riding the F train
one bright fall day
I saw a curling gush of gray
billowing out of a tower.
Glinting metal rain
fell on the train, the borough.
The sky is black now with the debris
of the blown-up world,
falling falling over us taking years.
The big man put a piano roll in us,
his goons looking on,
and we, playerless instruments,
emit tinny paeans to his power
and marry the men
who like that music.
Who advance in nothing but the skin
they think is a uniform
and curse at those they trample under their feet
as immoral for falling there.
What can we know of them,
of the lies they put in the reservoirs
in the dead of night

so we will drink them in?

But we draw memories in also

like sea air. We have our dead our dead our dead:

speak to us from across time!

Tell us how to hide in our bodies!

Tell us, we beg you, what we should do.

Snapshot

Sometimes it's like a snapshot
of something in violent movement.

—Tomas Tranströmer

Your memories

of people pledging their love

ride the wave of the past;

they ride the wave then it breaks

and you're seeing the real world,

composed, in fact, of pieces

our brains tape together.

We see the seams. The pieces

of a day careen by,

like timbers in a flood,

each bearing a number,

on waves broken in fact against a life—

23. 870. 3. 20.

Like parts with no instructions.

Which should I catch?

The one where the dad

bought me that guitar?

The one where he said

he should never have

been so tender?

Should I look back,

frame and hang up

a drawing my child made

at age four?

Knocking at a forgotten door

is my life's work.
Hawking my love in a basket,
like churros and mango slices
in ziplock bags
the woman sells in the F train station.
When that which is within us
spurs us on—
Don't miss that train!
—yearning pushes
the earth and our bodies
toward one another,
toward the masked future
that will herd us into its chambers.
Right now we're pelagic,
soaring over the sea of grief
that we don't know how to land in,
the patience we drape in worn thin
as an only dress: what is it
that we in fact have? The idea—
most lives don't matter.
The acts that erupt from it.

The Red Thread of Your Life

Destined as you are to contain a cataract
in a thimble, you can go out into the night
and meet the meanings of the words
as they come naked out of the station
and gather them into your coat,
them and all the rest no one talks about anymore.
The hopes of peoples. The gifts of the least.
The cruelty of the powerful.
They've only been waiting
to be wrapped in your thoughts of them
as in a warm salt sea; they are sick
from wanting it for so long.
It's your fate to have to stuff a whole language
into the tiny holder or opening you are given
while at the same time your soul gapes,
waiting for a bite of a love cake
that is all sweetness,
no frosting of mistrust
or anger-flavored chips in the layers.
The moon, pale stoplight you look up at,
holds out its wan warning: no such love exists!
but everyone keeps going.
Men keep being talked about;
women keep talking about men.
The sharp fingers of the fan palms
don't stop quivering, making nervous,
silent *Don't say it!* signs behind our backs
in a different country. Aging

keeps pushing the marks
that were contained on the inside
out to the surface to show the world:
See! I am fragile! I am naked as thoughts.
As branches that reach to each other like dendrites,
a streetlight round as a planet on a pole
glowing dimly between them,
your life a text you began
and don't want to give up on.
You believed that if you moved
you would move in the wrong way
so you kept still. You the people kept still.
The naked thread of your life, your collective life,
frayed more with each turn away from the real
until now the illusion encompasses us so
we cannot bear to live or die.

Here and There

Out there the world and I
battered each other
with the falling water of our passions.
The people ran out of the way.
In here, in the huge old cemetery,
the towering old trees
have stripped themselves
of their coverings
to show their souls' black architecture.
"Your turn," they whisper as they sway,
so you look down at yourself
as you stop pretending.
Out there, the people and I
were busy watching the shows
the masters put on for us,
of ourselves become perfect
from living in their fantastical
world. In here, patches
of the thinnest stalks
float just above the snow
in an ochre blur.
Beyond the gates
we so longed to be as beloved
as the people in their world
that we paid the masters
to let us live there; we made gods
of what are truly only
small broken men,

gods with which none of us
in our ordinariness could compare.
First we came as those splendid young,
to admire the silver-pink bars
of sky on the western edge
that glint through the trees'
outreaching capillaries.
Next we came as the living
to hold to the faces of our dead
by standing quiet over silent stones
in which their names are carved.
Next we came as the dead—
nothing left to explain.
The Earth gave us.
The Earth takes us away.

www.ingramcontent.com/pod-product-compliance
Lightning Source LLC
La Vergne TN
LVHW041204080426
835511LV00006B/735